KWANZAA
A FAMILY AFFAIR

Other Avon Camelot Books by
Mildred Pitts Walter

HAVE A HAPPY . . .
A NOVEL ABOUT KWANZAA

MILDRED PITTS WALTER, whose *Justin and the Best Biscuits in the World* won the Coretta Scott King Award for Literature, is the author of many well-received books for young readers. She has been celebrating Kwanzaa since its inception and imparts many of her own experiences in this book as well as in her fiction book titled *Have a Happy . . . .* Ms. Walter, who speaks extensively at schools all over the country, lives in Denver, Colorado.

Avon Books are available at special quantity discounts for bulk purchases for sales promotions, premiums, fund raising or educational use. Special books, or book excerpts, can also be created to fit specific needs.

For details write or telephone the office of the Director of Special Markets, Avon Books, Dept. FP, 1350 Avenue of the Americas, New York, New York 10019, 1-800-238-0658.

KWANZAA
A FAMILY AFFAIR

MILDRED PITTS WALTER

AN AVON CAMELOT BOOK

AVON BOOKS
A division of
The Hearst Corporation
1350 Avenue of the Americas
New York, New York 10019

Text copyright © 1995 by Mildred Pitts Walter
Illustrations copyright © 1995 by Cheryl Carrington
Published by arrangement with William Morrow and Company, Inc.
Library of Congress Catalog Card Number: 94-75329
ISBN: 0-380-72735-8
RL: All Ages

First Avon Camelot Printing: November 1996

CAMELOT TRADEMARK REG. U.S. PAT. OFF. AND IN OTHER COUNTRIES, MARCA REGISTRADA,
HECHO EN U.S.A.

Printed in the U.S.A.

OPM 10 9 8 7 6 5 4 3 2 1

For those African-American families who find joy in letting their children know where they have come from, so that they can know where they are at the moment and where they are going.

The information in this book about Kwanzaa principles and symbols is derived from the work of Dr. Maulana Karenga, in particular his book *Kwanzaa: Origins, Concepts, and Practice* (Los Angeles: Kawaida Publications, 1977).

My sincere appreciation to Mary O'Neal for the idea of making the *kalah* game, and to Mona Clark, Anna-Maria Curm, Mary Folsom, Arnett Floyd, Izetta Rawls, Rose Shipp, my son Craig Walter, and Wauda Walls, whose help made this project possible. Special thanks to Marjorie Waters for her valuable assistance in editing the crafts, and to Yvonne Gakii Njogu for her help with the Swahili vocabulary.

CONTENTS

On the following pages you will find some suggestions to help you and your family create activities that have special meaning to *you*. You'll find suggestions for things to do each day of Kwanzaa, as well as further topics for discussion and a suggested reading list to help you enhance your activities. At the end of the book is a special crafts section that gives directions for making games, gifts, and the specific things you will need for the celebration. Recipes for foods that many African-Americans find special are also included. I hope you will find them special too.

Kwanzaa yenu iwe heri! Happy Kwanzaa!

WHAT IS KWANZAA?

Kwanzaa! A time for looking backward, for looking forward, and for having fun. For seven days many African-American homes are decorated in red, green, and black, and filled with the sounds of music, lively talk, and laughter. Family members and friends dress up in African garb, children dramatize historical characters, and everyone gets ready to have a great time remembering, singing, dancing, and sharing traditional foods.

Kwanzaa is an African-American celebration that begins on December 26 and lasts through January 1. Many African-American customs have their origins in the rich cultures of Africa, and the arts, rituals, and rites of those cultures offer uniquely appropriate ideas for Kwanzaa activities and ceremonies.

The word *Kwanzaa* comes from the Swahili word *kwanza*. Swahili is a language spoken in many areas of the African continent, but especially in East Africa. *Kwanza* means "first." It is part of the phrase *matunda ya kwanza,* which means "first fruits."

The African-American festival of Kwanzaa was founded by Dr. Maulana Karenga, executive director of the Institute of Pan-African Studies in Los Angeles and the leader of US, the black nationalist organization. Kwanzaa was first celebrated in 1966.

Because the holiday is so new, and because we African-Americans are such a varied people, there is no *one* way to celebrate the occasion. However, because all of us share a strong bond in struggle, the seven principles of Kwanzaa, called the *nguzo saba,* can provide common themes on which to base our celebrations. These seven principles are:

Unity
Self-determination
Collective work
Cooperative economics
Purpose
Creativity
Faith

Dr. Karenga says the concept of Kwanzaa "is derived from and inspired by the harvest celebrations of agricultural African peoples. . . . 'First fruits' celebrations were traditional throughout Africa. . . ." People gave thanks for the first fruits of their harvests and for their achievement through working together. Even though African-Americans are now mostly an urban people, with no crops to harvest, Kwanzaa was founded to provide an opportunity for us to celebrate a season's yield of personal and group achievements and to stress our cultural roots in Africa. The celebration is a rededication of our efforts toward even greater achievements and more meaningful lives in the future.

In many parts of Africa, people hold special ceremonies before planting or harvesting their crops. Jomo Kenyatta, in his book *Facing Mt. Kenya,* tells of a planting ritual that takes place in Kenya, East Africa:

> The Gikuyu elders arrange for a planting ceremony immediately after the rain falls. Seeds from maize, millet, and a variety of beans are selected. These seeds along with the stomach of a lamb that has been sacrificed are placed into seed-calabashes. They are then handed over to a woman chosen from women who qualify for the position of "Mother" of the community. This woman takes the seeds to her hut to keep them overnight.

The sticks from a sacred tree, sharpened with the sacrificial knife and least affected by the fire that roasted the lamb, are given to two children who had taken part in a sacrifice for rain. These two children along with the elders who will participate in the planting ceremony will also sleep in the hut.

Early the next morning the children are called to go out and reenter the hut. This custom of choosing who will first go out to enter a house is a very important one to the Gikuyu people. It is believed that if the one chosen goes out or enters first, then the household will have good luck. If one who is not chosen enters, that can bring ill luck. After the early morning ceremony the elders, woman and children go out to a special field to perform the ritual of planting the seeds. On the way no one is allowed to speak to or touch the people participating in the ceremony. When they arrive in the field, the leading elder takes the calabashes. Holding the calabash of maize seeds and facing Mt. Kenya (*Kere Nyaga,* the mountain of mystery), the elder offers a prayer. Then the maize seeds are given to the woman. She, in turn, gives them to the children, who plant them with the special digging sticks. The ritual is repeated with all the other seed-calabashes until all the seeds have been planted. When the elders, the woman, and the children return to the homestead, a planting horn is then sounded to tell the people of the community that the ceremony is now over. They can go about planting their own fields.

In West Africa—in parts of Mali and Senegal, and all over The Gambia—there are celebrations for planting and harvesting. When I visited The Gambia, I learned a special dance and song used at harvest time to celebrate the strongest man—the one who has worked hardest in the fields. To decide who this is, the men perform a dance, during which they make their muscles so taut that a very hard knife stab will not go through the muscle.

During the harvest, the women go into the fields to help collect the produce and bring it back to the compounds. Then all the people in the village come out to celebrate the harvest and the strongest man. While everyone dances a special dance, the name of the strongest man is called in a special song.

The dances and songs that I learned in The Gambia reminded me of some dances we African-Americans do. For example, African-American circle and line dances, in which one person or couple performs alone, creating improvised movements while the people forming the line or circle urge them on, are similar to many African dances. Of course, we don't have African drums, nor do we have the planting and harvesting rituals. We do, however, have the music and rhythms that originated in the drumbeats of West Africa.

We also have the idea of the extended family, reverence for our elders, and an abiding religious faith— all of which are important in Africa. Remember this heritage and use it to make your Kwanzaa celebrations meaningful and happy.

KWANZAA PRINCIPLES, SYMBOLS, AND RITUALS

Though the Kwanzaa celebration has its roots in African traditions, it is definitely an African-American idea designed to bring African-Americans together. There are seven principles, or ideas, around which Kwanzaa activities can be organized. These ideas are clearly American, but *we* are both African and American, shaped by both cultures, so the principles are expressed in the Swahili language.

In Swahili, the seven principles are called the *nguzo saba*. They are:

1. **UMOJA** (*unity*)
   Working together with family, community, nation, and race.

2. **KUJICHAGULIA** (*self-determination*)
   Defining ourselves, renaming ourselves,
   speaking for ourselves, planning for ourselves.

3. **UJIMA** (*collective work and responsibility*)
   Building our communities, sharing and
   solving our problems.

4. **UJAMAA** (*cooperative economics*)
   Building and maintaining our own stores and
   other businesses, and profiting from them
   together.

5. **NIA** (*purpose*)
   Striving to build our communities and to do
   again the things that will restore our traditional
   values: respect for our elders, respect for one
   another, responsibility for ourselves and one
   another.

6. **KUUMBA** (*creativity*)
   Using our minds and hands to make our communities more beautiful than they were when
   we inherited them. Using our hands to make
   gifts that record and keep alive our history.

7. **IMANI** (*faith*)
   Believing with all our hearts in our people, our
   parents, our elders, and our teachers, and in
   the righteousness and inevitable victory of our
   struggle for equality.

Symbols are used in the Kwanzaa celebration. Symbols are things that *can* be seen and touched, and which represent things that *cannot* be seen and touched. A flag is a symbol. It is a piece of material used to represent a country.

A ritual is a special way of performing a ceremony. It can also be called a rite, or a collective act, as in a religious service. Have you ever been to a wedding, a baby christening or naming ceremony, or a funeral? Those are all rituals.

There are seven basic symbols used to perform the rituals in the Kwanzaa celebration. These are also named in Swahili. They are:

1. **KIKOMBE CHA UMOJA** (*unity cup*)
   This special cup holds the drink that is used to honor our ancestors in a toast. After the toast to the ancestors, all members of the family drink from this cup.
2. **KINARA** (*candle holder*)
   This symbolizes our very first ancestors, man and woman, the makers of our people and principles.
3. **MAZAO** (*crops*)
   These represent our connection with African peoples who celebrate the planting and harvesting of foods. Crops can also remind us

of our productivity; of our having worked
together to achieve our goals for the year.

4. **MISHUMAA SABA** (*seven candles*)

The seven candles symbolize the seven
principles. The black candle in the center of
the *kinara,* or candle holder, stands for African
peoples; the three red candles stand for our
struggle; and the three green ones stand for
our young people.

5. **MKEKA** (*woven mat*)

The mat is a symbol of tradition and history.
Who we are and what we do are tightly woven
together.

6. **VIBUNZI** (*ears of corn*)

Each ear of corn represents a child in the
family. Each kernel of corn represents
generations of children to come.

7. **ZAWADI** (*gifts*)

These are symbols of commitments kept by
children and promises kept by parents. Gifts
are given with our struggle in mind. The best
gifts are documents of our history (books,
paintings, sculpture) and things made with
our creative minds and hands.

There is another symbol: the *bendera* (black, red, and
green flag). The flag was first used by Marcus Garvey,

a leader from Jamaica who started the "Back to Africa" movement in the 1920s. The colors represent the same things as the colors of the *mishumaa saba,* or seven candles. The flag is displayed during the week of celebration.

Now that you know the principles and the symbols, you can plan activities for the rituals—lighting the candles, pouring a libation for our ancestors, taking a drink to honor ancestors of your immediate family and national ancestors who are well known—and give meaning to the principles. Doing these things will make Kwanzaa a meaningful experience for you, your family, and your friends.

Do Your Own Thing

Kwanzaa is, especially, a family affair. The success of a Kwanzaa celebration depends on the imaginative planning and creative participation of every family member. Many of us review our histories so that we will know who we are, from where we have come, and how we can shape our futures. Families remember ancestors and celebrate the personal achievements of their members—and the contributions African-Americans have made to the history of the community, the city, the state, and the nation.

It is a time to emphasize traditions and values. Your family may have a special way of welcoming and naming new babies. There may be a particular thing you do, or once did, on holidays. For example, in the family of one of my friends, all the men visit every household of theirs on Christmas Eve. The children look forward to those visits, for they hear true stories about the family and receive many gifts. Each house, in turn, prepares a treat for the men: a drink, or small servings of food or sweets. The eldest man begins the visits. When he leaves a house, the men of the house join him. This is repeated over and over until all the houses have been visited. The men then end their visits in the home of the elder. Remembering traditions like this one, even if they are no longer practiced, gives us a sense of our family's history and values.

Kwanzaa is also a time to shed light on our *shared history*. We have national traditions and holidays that have meaning to all African-Americans, such as Black History Month and Martin Luther King, Jr.'s Birthday. Many of us celebrate the Nineteenth of June, the day in 1863 on which slaves in Texas and Louisiana learned about the Emancipation Proclamation (which had become effective on January 1, 1863).

Families throughout the community can come together to celebrate their shared ancestors, especially those who gave their lives for our freedom. Kwanzaa is a good time to renew our commitment to the struggle for equality, and to celebrate ourselves and our collective achievements. These seven days are a joyous reminder that we have, against many odds, remained a strong, creative, and jubilant people.

Much of African-American history is a story of struggle without material wealth. Many of us come to Kwanzaa having, by necessity, to use our talents to make a bountiful and joyous celebration within a limited budget. But gifts, symbols, and much of the food required can be made with household resources, creative minds, and willing hands. Planning activities and making things for the celebration may continue year-round.

My family starts by saving as many decorations as possible for the next year. We save outstanding schoolwork that can be laminated, paintings by young family members that can be framed—we are always looking for little things that will bring meaning to our Kwanzaa celebration.

Each of the seven days of Kwanzaa requires special preparation, and the rituals require specific items:

1. a candle holder
2. seven candles
    (one black, three green, and three red)
3. a table
4. a flag
5. a special cup

6. several colorful ears of corn
7. a basket of fruits and vegetables
8. a mat for the table
9. gifts, preferably handmade

Families can have fun making most of these items, just as they have fun preparing for any celebration. Remember how much fun it is to plan for Halloween—making costumes, carving pumpkins? You can have as much fun making Kwanzaa symbols.

Your *kinara* (candle holder) must hold seven candles, but what it looks like—its design, color, and size—should be decided by the family. The *mkeka* (woven mat for the table) brings a special traditional meaning to Kwanzaa. It is an important symbol of our African heritage, and of our togetherness as families and communities. It can be woven from ribbon, paper, string, plaited rope, tie-dyed cloth, or any number of things.

Many wonderful gifts can also be made that remind us of our heritage: African masks and games, audiotapes of family memories, or books can become *zawadi*. Use your imagination!

Getting your family's oral history on tape will not only help you know yourself better, but it can also be great fun. Make an appointment to interview your elders. Then write down what you want to ask them.

Special memories are personal, so your questions can be personal: Where were they born? What were their parents like? What was it like when they were young? You may want to know where, how, and when your grandfather met your grandmother. Were they married right away? Did they both work? What did they do? Did they have their own house, or did they live with their parents? You may want to ask questions about the family's health history.

A book from your taped interviews of memories can be used at Kwanzaa celebrations again and again. You may want to illustrate it or find photographs that make the memories come even more alive.

Games make wonderful gifts, and some are very easy to make. One such game is *kalah,* which originated in Africa. You may know this game by another name, for many African peoples have their own name for it.

A quilt is a very special, oftentimes cooperative, creation. Quilts are usually heirlooms that are lasting and give good service. One for a new baby or a family wall hanging is an extended project, but it is well worth the effort. Putting different colors and pieces together to make a pattern is lots of fun that the whole family can share. It is even more fun to see how scraps of worn-out clothing can become a usable work of art.

You may want to ask an elder in the family to tell you about quilting in her day. When I was a child, there were quilting bees. Sometimes as many as six women worked at the same time on a quilt. What fun we had during this party. My friends and I sat under the quilt, listening to the women talk. They told wonderful stories, and sometimes they would forget we were under there and blurt out a bit of gossip not meant for our ears.

Kwanzaa is a good time to share food with friends. Food is used in many cultures to welcome strangers and to break barriers. In Russia bread is broken with strangers to show friendship. The kola nut is shared to welcome guests in many African countries; and in China tea is served.

Sharing food is a long-standing African and African-American tradition. In Africa, people often walk long distances to visit. They are tired, hungry, and thirsty when they reach their destination; therefore the host always has food and drink prepared for his guests' arrival.

Prior to the 1960s, here in the United States, because of segregation laws, African-Americans had to travel long distances without being able to stay in hotels or eat in restaurants near the highway. We stopped in the homes of friends, or of friends of friends we did not know, to rest. They welcomed us with food and drink.

Kwanzaa is a good time to bring out traditional recipes and give the history of ingredients used by grandmothers or other relatives to make memorable occasions special. I can remember how my mother, my sisters, and I, on Christmas Eve, pulled out all the recipes and worked from early morning until late that night making cakes, cookies, and pies. What fun we had deciding which cake to make next and who would mix the batter and who would put on the icing. Such fun can be had making Kwanzaa symbols.

Try to find an African dish for each day of Kwanzaa. I have included two African recipes: peanut-and-rice pudding from The Gambia, West Africa, home country of the ancestors of the late Alex Haley, author of the book *Roots,* and benne wafers.

Benne means sesame in Mandingo, a West African language. Captured Africans are believed to have introduced sesame to North America perhaps as early as the 1600s. Today African-American cooks still use this seed in cookies, breads, stews, and other foods. Eating sesame seeds is said to bring good luck.

I have also included two African-American recipes: yam chips, and ambrosia. Yams are a staple food in many African countries. We use a similar food, called the sweet potato. The sweet potato was so important to our diet that the noted scientist George Washington Carver developed more than one hundred products from the plant. You will enjoy this unusual treat whether you sprinkle the chips with salt and pepper or with sugar and cinnamon. I like them best with sugar and cinnamon. Ambrosia is a favorite in many of our homes and is often served on festive occasions. You will find it easy to make. It tastes good and it's colorful.

Plan ahead!

Remember, you don't wait until the hour of the birthday celebration to bake the cake, nor until Christmas Day to buy the tree and the gifts. So it is with Kwanzaa. Start early, say in the month of September. In the late fall buy colorful ears of corn, one to represent each child in the family. These, if wrapped carefully and stored away, can be used year after year.

Making things to use in the celebration adds special meaning and can keep the principle of creativity alive all year long. Kwanzaa is a family affair! Work with your parents or another adult. At the end of the book are some suggested craft activities that call for inexpensive materials that can be found in most homes or purchased in discount stores or supermarkets. They are suggestions only. Do your own thing in your own way! Work together. Then, by December 26, everything you need for the ceremony will be ready.

CREATING A JOYOUS CELEBRATION

At least two weeks before the Kwanzaa celebration begins, send invitations to friends and family stating the time your ceremony will start on December 26. Consider inviting friends who have never been part of a Kwanzaa celebration, or distant relatives who may not have been included in family gatherings before. Kwanzaa offers a good opportunity to renew family ties and make new friends.

Now is the time to decide just how festive you want your Kwanzaa to be. Some families decorate the room with black, red, and green balloons. People may wear African clothing such as a *bui-bui* (elegant gown for women) with a matching *gele* (head wrap), a *dashiki* (loose-fitting shirt or blouse), or a *kanzu* (robe for men). Some serve a full meal before or after the ceremony. Others serve only simple refreshments such as fruit, juice, and cheese and crackers for the first six days, knowing that the seventh day will end with a *karamu* (feast).

Spend time deciding exactly how your ceremony will proceed. Also decide which family members will participate in each part of the ceremony.

Soon December 26, the first day of Kwanzaa, will arrive. Before your guests come, set all the symbols on a low table: the *mkeka* (mat), the *kinara* (candle holder) with the *mishumaa saba* (candles—three red ones on the right, three green ones on the left, and a black one in the middle), the *kikombe cha umoja* (unity cup), the *vibunzi* (ears of corn), the *mazao* (fruits and vegetables), and the *zawadi* (gifts).

After all the guests have arrived, the ceremony can begin. Remember, this is a celebration of you and your family, so you want your ceremony to have special meaning for you. Included are some suggestions for activities for each of the seven days. You may want to try some of them.

Each day of Kwanzaa, before the ritual begins, welcome your guests, wishing them *Kwanzaa yenu iwe heri* (Happy Kwanzaa).

Name and briefly explain the seven principles of

Kwanzaa (see pages 17-18). This can be done by one person, or family members can take turns.

Name and explain the symbols of Kwanzaa (see pages 19-20). This, too, can be done by one person, or family members can take turns.

Greeting: *Habari gani?*
(What's the news? or What's happening?)
Response: *Umoja.*

An elder member of the family pours a *tambiko* (libation or drink) from the *kikombe cha umoja* (unity cup), in honor of our ancestors. In Africa, where most ceremonies are held outside, libations are poured into the earth, but you may use a small container to receive your libation. After pouring the libation, the elder raises the unity cup and praises the ancestors, then drinks from the cup and passes it on. Guests may choose to drink or simply to pass the cup on. Those who drink call the name of a family ancestor or an outstanding African-American and identify that person (for example, "Fannie Lou Hamer—a sister who challenged injustice in the state of Mississippi").

Light the black candle, which represents African-American people and unity. Then explain what unity means to your family. If you have made a book of your family history, you may want to read from it at this time to symbolize unity in the history of your family.

The next part of the ceremony is up to you. Some families enjoy performing skits or recalling family stories that demonstrate the principle of the day. Here is one way to proceed: Invite each person to speak about what unity means to him or her. One person might talk about how members of the community have worked together to help solve a neighborhood problem, or helped someone in need. Another might suggest something that the family can do together to improve their feeling of unity. No one needs to speak for very long. The entire ceremony usually lasts about thirty minutes, at which time the candle is put out.

Follow the ceremony with refreshments, which can be anything from simple snacks to a full meal, and the giving of gifts.

SECOND DAY
KUJICHAGULIA (*self-determination*)
Greeting: *Habari gani?*
Response: *Kujichagulia.*

Perform the libation ceremony, again naming an ancestor as you receive the cup. Try to name different ancestors each night.

Relight the black candle, then light the first candle to its right. Explain what self-determination means to your family.

Invite each person to tell what self-determination means to him or her. Then proceed with your own program. Some families enjoy choosing African names for themselves at this ceremony. Some like to perform a skit that demonstrates African-American self-determination, such as reenacting a sit-in or an attempt to register to vote in the South.

Serve refreshments and exchange gifts.

THIRD DAY
UJIMA (*collective work and responsibility*)
Greeting: *Habari gani?*
Response: *Ujima.*

Perform the libation ceremony.

Relight the black candle and the first one to its right. Then light the first candle to the left and explain what collective work and responsibility means to your family.

The program tonight might include telling stories of how African-Americans have worked together to achieve a collective goal, or you may let younger members of the family dramatize how responsibility works in their everyday activities at home or at school.

Serve refreshments and exchange gifts.

FOURTH DAY
UJAMAA (*cooperative economics*)
Greeting: *Habari gani?*
Response: *Ujamaa.*

Perform the libation ceremony.

Relight the candles for the first three days; then light the second candle on the right and explain what cooperative economics means to your family.

Tonight's activities might include talking about the importance of a savings account, or role-playing a job interview. You could compile a list of African-American businesses in your community.

Serve refreshments and exchange gifts.

FIFTH DAY
NIA (*purpose*)

Greeting: *Habari gani?*
Response: *Nia*

Perform the libation ceremony.

Relight the candles for the first four days; then light the second candle on the left and explain what purpose means to your family.

Tonight's program could include reading aloud about the ancient African empires. Use the reading to spark discussion about our commitment to know more about our African heritage and our traditional values of respect for our elders, respect for one another, and our responsibility for ourselves and each other. You might want to share some African folktales or sing African-American freedom songs.

Serve refreshments and exchange gifts.

SIXTH DAY
KUUMBA (creativity)

Greeting: *Habari gani?*
Response: *Kuumba.*

Perform the libation ceremony.

Relight the candles for the first five days; then light the third candle on the right and explain what creativity means to your family.

Tonight's program can be especially fun. You may want to prepare for it by learning some African dances or practicing on African musical instruments, making African masks, creating a song, writing a poem, or painting a picture that illustrates one of the Kwanzaa principles. At the ceremony you may share your creation. You might also want to recite something by one of the great African-American poets, such as Langston Hughes or Maya Angelou. Or share picture books written and illustrated by African-Americans. Or listen to music by African and African-American musicians.

Serve refreshments and exchange gifts.

SEVENTH DAY
IMANI (*faith*)
Greeting: *Habari gani?*
Response: *Imani.*

Perform the libation ceremony.

Relight the candles for the first six days; then light the last candle and explain what faith means to your family.

Like other winter festivals—Christmas, Hanukkah, Las Posadas—Kwanzaa celebrates the spirit of sharing. The seventh day is also the beginning of a new year— a new season of faith, commitment, and renewal. You may want to get together with other families for a joint ceremony and celebration. Traditionally the food for the last day is plentiful and includes many African, Caribbean, and African-American dishes. Perhaps you'll want to plan a potluck feast. Encourage everyone to prepare a traditional dish and wear colorful African garments.

The ceremony follows the pattern set on previous nights, and the program often includes music, dancing, and storytelling. The evening ends with everyone committing to unity by saying *"Harambee!"* This means "Pull together." Then an elder makes a statement of farewell, called *tamshi la tutaonana.*

Things may not all go exactly as planned, but if everyone does his or her best, then the spirit of

Kwanzaa will reign! Being able to improvise is a wonderful part of the African-American tradition. At the last celebration I attended, the elder who was to open the ceremony was delayed. We waited and waited. Then we learned that he was unable to come. Another elder who had never attended a Kwanzaa ceremony before was taken aside and given some fast instructions. He did a beautiful job, and no one was aware that he had not done it before. When it looks like things aren't going well, just step up and do your thing. Create your own celebration, and you'll have a truly historic time and lots of fun.

MAKING SYMBOLS, GIFTS, AND FOOD FOR KWANZAA

The following crafts call for inexpensive materials that are found in most homes or that can be purchased in discount stores and supermarkets. Keep in mind that Kwanzaa is a family affair. Work with your parents or another adult.

Read the directions all the way through and make sure that you have everything you need to complete the project before you start. Never begin a project without a parent's permission.

MAKING SYMBOLIC GIFTS
AND FOOD FOR KWANZAA

SYMBOLS

KINARA

A *kinara* is a holder for seven candles, one for each day of Kwanzaa. It is the centerpiece of the holiday, so making a *kinara* together as a family is especially meaningful. Directions for two different *kinaras* are given here. One is made with plaster of paris; it is a favorite of mine, but it may not be a good idea if you have never worked with this material before. The other *kinara* is made of a flour-based clay, which is more forgiving, and a material young children love to work with. Both *kinaras* can be stored and used again, year after year.

PLASTER OF PARIS KINARA

This *kinara* is long and narrow, with a raised section in the middle to hold the black candle. Three red candles stand on one side, and three green candles stand on the other. The base of this *kinara* is 14 inches long and about 2 inches tall; the raised center is about 5 inches tall. The *kinara* is designed for standard commercial candles. By adjusting the size of the molds, you can change the dimensions if you want, but make sure your *kinara* is big enough to hold the candles.

Because the plaster sets so quickly, this is not an easy one-person project. Try to get the whole family involved, especially in making the candle holes, which needs to be done quickly. Give everybody an apron or old shirt to protect his or her clothes. New garbage bags make great coveralls if they're cut at the bottom for the neck and at the sides for the arms. Spread newspapers on the table and floor where you're working, too.

Before you start, read the instructions all the way through so you can move quickly once you begin.

WHAT YOU NEED:

    10 lbs. of plaster of paris (a powdered plaster you
        can find at art-supply or hardware stores)
    3 one-quart milk cartons, clean and dry
    7 standard-size commercial candles
    (3 red, 3 green, 1 black)
    large mixing bowl or bucket
    scissors
    stapler
    old newspapers
    ruler, at least 15 inches long
    poster paints (optional)

WHAT YOU DO:

1. Open the top of two milk cartons. With scissors, cut the tops off at the crease.

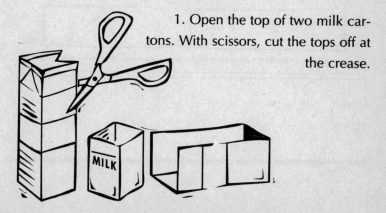

2. Cut one side off each carton. If you accidentally slice into the carton, use clear plastic tape to repair the damage.

3. Make the mold for the base by putting one carton inside the other, overlapping about ½ inch. The bottoms of the two cartons should be opposite each other, 14 inches apart. Tape the seams together with plastic tape.

4. Make the mold for the raised center by cutting the third milk carton into a square tube 3 inches long, open at both ends. Set it aside.

5. Dust the insides of the base mold with a little dry plaster of paris. Shake out any excess plaster. Set the mold on the table with the open side up. Put the ruler down on the table next to it, and have the candles nearby.

6. Mix about 2 quarts of plaster. Follow the directions on the package until the plaster is the consistency of heavy cream.

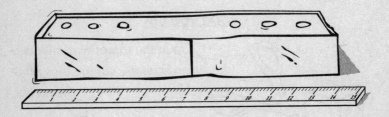

7. Pour the liquid plaster into the base mold to about ½ inch from the edge of the mold. (Somebody should throw out any leftover plaster and clean the bucket while other members of the family work on the candle holes.)

8. As soon as the plaster is poured, make the candle holes. Use the ruler to locate the candle holes as shown. Insert the base of a candle about 1 inch deep into the plaster, and remove it quickly.

9. Keep inserting and removing the candles as the plaster hardens, and rotate the candle bases slightly so the hole is a little bigger than the candle. The plaster will dry in minutes, so make the candle holes quickly. If you have six people around, each can take one candle and make one candle hole.

10. Make 1 quart of fresh plaster.

11. When the base is dry, two people should work together to make the raised center of the *kinara*. One centers the square tube on the base and holds it firmly down on the plaster, making sure the tube is inside the lip of the base mold. The other person pours the plaster into the tube, and then makes the seventh candle hole while the plaster hardens. The mold must be held firmly in place during this process.

12. Let the *kinara* stand for a day or so, to get completely

hard. Then cut away the mold. You can leave the *kinara* as is, for a nice, homemade look. Or you can sand it for a smoother finish, and then paint it with a design you like.

BREAD-DOUGH KINARA

This "bread dough" is really a flour-based clay, not the beginning of a loaf of bread. The ingredients are readily available, and the clay is easy to work with, even for young children.

WHAT YOU NEED:

½ cup salt
¾ cup boiling water
2 cups nonrising whole-wheat flour
  (*not* self-rising flour)
1 tablespoon vegetable oil
  cookie sheet
  aluminum foil

7 standard-sized commercial candles
   (3 red, 3 green, 1 black)
   poster paints (optional)

WHAT YOU DO:

1. Put the salt in a big mixing bowl. Add the water, and stir to dissolve the salt. Let cool for 5 minutes.
2. Add the flour and oil to the bowl.
3. Mix the dough with a spoon, then with your hands once the ingredients are blended.
4. Knead the dough with your hands until it is smooth. Keep wetting your hands as you work so the dough doesn't stick to your skin.
5. Preheat oven to 300 degrees.
6. Divide the dough roughly into half, and roll one half into a smooth ball. Set the other half aside.
7. With the palms of your hands, roll the ball of dough back and forth on the countertop to form a "snake" about 12 inches long and 3 inches thick. Curve the snake into an S shape. This is the base of the *kinara*. (You can change the dimensions if you want, as long as the final shape is long and narrow, and big enough to hold 7 candles.)

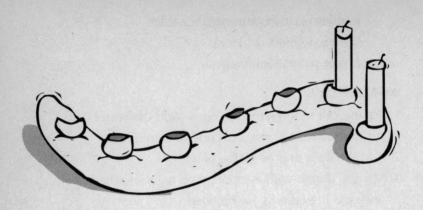

8. Set the kinara base on the foil-covered cookie sheet, and tidy the S curve if you need to.

9. Break the remaining dough into 7 equal-sized lumps, and roll each one into a smooth ball.

10. Press a candle down into each of the 7 balls, deep enough so the candle remains upright on its own. Place the 7 balls on the base, spacing them equally, and push them down onto the base so that they stay put and the candles stand straight.

11. Wet your hands, then shape and smooth the kinara until you like the way it looks. Move the candles around to widen the holes a little, as they will close slightly during baking. Then carefully remove the candles.

12. Bake the *kinara* about 2 hours, or until it looks dry.

13. After baking, the *kinara* will be sand colored. You can leave it as is, or paint it with water-soluble poster paints.

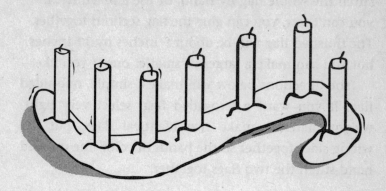

NOTE: If you have leftover dough, you can use it to make beads for a necklace. Roll pieces of dough into ovals or balls between your palms. When you are happy with the size and shape, use a skewer or small nail to make a hole through the center of each bead. You can bake the beads with the *kinara,* but they may be done sooner because they are smaller. Paint the finished beads with your favorite colors, and string them on yarn or heavy thread.

BENDERA

This version of Marcus Garvey's flag is a very simple project for people with basic sewing skills. You can stitch the whole flag by hand, or use a machine. If you can't sew, you can glue the flag sections together. The finished flag will be about 9 inches by 11 inches, but you can make a larger or smaller one if you like.

The directions below will make a simple, one-sided flag. If you want a two-sided flag, select very light-weight material, make two identical flags, put the wrong sides together so the bands of color line up, and hand-stitch the two flags together.

WHAT YOU NEED:

- 1 piece of lightweight black fabric, 3½ by 12 inches
- 1 piece of lightweight red fabric, 3½ by 12 inches
- 1 piece of lightweight green fabric, 3½ by 12 inches
- ½-inch dowel, about 2 feet long
- scissors
- common pins
- needle and thread, or sewing machine
- iron
- stapler

WHAT YOU DO:

1. Lay the black cloth rectangle on the red one so they match exactly. (Some fabric looks the same on both

sides. If yours does not, make sure the right sides face each other.)

2. By hand or machine, sew the black and red rectangles along one long side, with a ¼-inch seam allowance.

3. Unfold the flag, and lay it on a table so the seam is underneath. Pin the green fabric to the other long side of the black fabric, right sides together.

4. Sew the black and green rectangles together with a ¼-inch seam allowance.

5. Press the seams with an iron so they lie flat. Press the

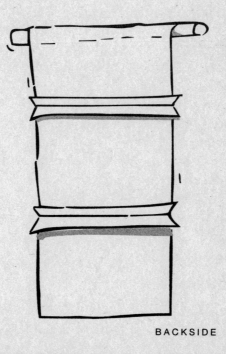

BACKSIDE

outside edges of the flag under about ¼ inch, then turn again so the raw edge does not show. Stitch the hem by hand, all the way around the flag.

6. With the red fabric on top, roll the left edge of the flag around the dowel, and staple or glue the fabric in place. (If you prefer, turn the left edge of the flag under and stitch it down to create a channel for the dowel. If the flag slides down the dowel, a single staple should hold it in place.)

MKEKA

You can make a *mkeka* from cloth, string, paper, or other materials. The instructions below use satin ribbon, which is inexpensive and easy to work with, and weaves beautifully. The different-width ribbons give the *mkeka* an interesting pattern.

You can change the ribbon widths if you want; the wider the ribbons, the more quickly the project will go.

WHAT YOU NEED:

8 yards of ⅞-inch black ribbon
8 yards of ⅝-inch red ribbon
12 yards of ⅝-inch green ribbon
white glue
scissors
ruler

WHAT YOU DO:

1. Cut 18 lengths of green ribbon each 23 inches long.
2. Cut 1 length of black ribbon 15 inches long.
3. With a pencil, make a mark 1½ inches from the end of the black ribbon.
4. Put a dab of glue on the tip of one green ribbon. Glue it to the 15-inch black ribbon at the pencil mark, as shown.

5. Glue a second green ribbon to the black one, close enough to touch but not overlap the first green ribbon. Continue until all the green ribbons are glued to the black one.
6. Cut 23 lengths of red ribbon each 12 inches long. Cut 8 lengths of black ribbon each 12 inches long. Cut 1 length of black ribbon 25 inches long.
7. With a pencil, make a mark 1½ inches from the end of the 25-inch black ribbon.
8. Put a dab of glue on the tip of one red ribbon. Glue it to the 25-inch black ribbon at the pencil mark.

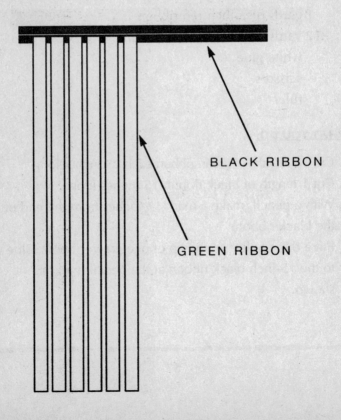

BLACK RIBBON

GREEN RIBBON

9. Glue a 12-inch black ribbon next to the red ribbon.
10. Glue 3 red ribbons next to the black one.
11. Continue gluing ribbons to the 25-inch black ribbon in this order: 1 black, 3 red, 1 black, 3 red, and so on, until all the 12-inch red and black ribbons are glued to the 25-inch black ribbon. The last two ribbons in the pattern should be 1 black and 1 red.
12. When the glue is dry, lay the black and red ribbons on a flat surface, glued sides up, loose ends facing you. Lay the green ribbons, glued sides up, perpendicular to and on top of the red and black ones.

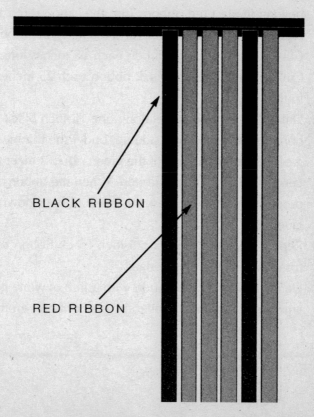

BLACK RIBBON

RED RIBBON

13. Starting at the corner where the black ribbon edges meet, weave the top green ribbon over and under the red and black ribbons.

14. Alternating the over-and-under pattern, weave the second green ribbon through the red and black ribbons.

15. Continue until all the green ribbons are woven through the red and black ribbons. When you finish, there will be two edges of fringe. Straighten and tighten the ribbons so the *mkeka* lies flat, and the ribbon is as straight as you can make it.

16. Trim the exposed green ends to a straight line ½ inch beyond the last red ribbon. Trim the exposed red and black ribbons to ½ inch beyond the last green ribbon.

17. Cut 3 lengths of black ribbon each 15 inches long. Cut 3 more lengths of black ribbon each 25 inches long.

18. Dab a line of white glue along one 15-inch black ribbon, and slide it, glued side up, under the trimmed green edges so the tips of the green ribbons meet the center line of the black ribbon. When the ribbons are properly positioned, press the green ribbons down to glue them in place.

19. Repeat step 18 to glue a 25-inch black ribbon to the trimmed red and black edges.

20. Dab a 15-inch black ribbon with a line of white glue, and position it directly over the black ribbon on the

short side of the *mkeka*. Press the ribbon into place. Repeat for the remaining three sides, gluing the remaining black ribbons in place. This will frame the *mkeka* top and bottom, so you can use either side.

21. When the glue is dry, trim the black-ribbon frame so the *mkeka* has neat, square corners.

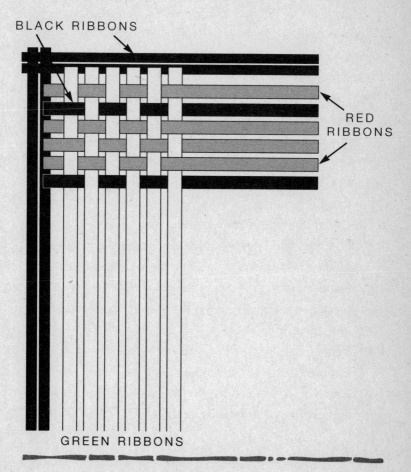

BLACK RIBBONS

RED RIBBONS

GREEN RIBBONS

GIFTS

KALAH

Almost every African culture plays some version of this two-person game, though it is called different names, such as *mancala* or *awari*. Simple versions can be played by children as young as five, but the more skill and experience you have, the more complex and demanding the game is.

The game board can be put together in a few minutes with materials you will probably find around the house.

WHAT YOU NEED:

> egg carton, with lid
> scissors
> tape or stapler
> 36 counters (pebbles, beans, macaroni, or other items that are small and easy to pick up)

WHAT YOU DO:

1. With scissors, cut the lid off the egg carton.
2. Cut the lid in half, across its width.
3. Tape or staple one lid-half to one end of the egg carton, to make a tray. Repeat with the remaining lid-half at the opposite end of the carton. These trays are called *kalahs*.

HOW TO PLAY:

1. The players sit across from each other, with the *kalah*

board between them. The row of 6 spaces in front of you, and the *kalah* to the right, are yours. The opposite spaces, and the *kalah* to the left, are your opponent's.

2. Put 3 counters in each of your 6 spaces, while your opponent puts 3 counters in each of his spaces. (As your skill improves, you may use more counters. Experts start with 6 counters in each space.)

3. The object of the game is to collect the most counters in your *kalah*. To begin, pick up all the counters in one of your spaces. Moving counter clockwise, put one counter in each of the next spaces you come to. You can put a counter in your own *kalah*, but if, later in the game, you reach your opponent's *kalah*, skip it and put the counter in the next space.

4. If the last counter in your hand lands in your *kalah*, take another turn. Otherwise it is your opponent's turn.

5. You can capture each other's counters. If your last counter lands in one of your opponent's empty spaces, take all the counters in the opposite space and put them in your *kalah*.

6. When one player's spaces are empty, the other player—the one whose spaces are not empty—moves all the remaining counters to his *kalah*. Then each player tallies the number of counters in his *kalah*, and the one with the most wins.

AFRICAN MASK

Throughout Africa, people make masks out of local materials to use in rituals. This version of an African mask is made of papier-mâché, which is strips of newspaper and paste, layered on a balloon and allowed to dry for several days. It is a little messy—wear aprons or old clothes—but the mess is easy to clean up, and even young children can work with this material. If you want, you can do some research and try to decorate your mask in the style of a particular African people.

WHAT YOU NEED:

newspaper
large pot or double boiler
large wooden mixing spoon
wheat paste
1 cup nonrising wheat flour (not self-rising flour)
¼ cup sugar
1 quart warm water
1 cup cold water
large, oval party balloon
drinking glass
pin or needle
scissors (optional)
poster paints

Note: *This recipe will make enough paste for 3 or 4 large masks. The paste can't be stored, so if you want a smaller batch, cut the recipe in half. When you are finished, throw away any leftover paste.*

WHAT YOU DO:

1. Take 5 or 6 double sheets of a full-size newspaper. If you use the comics or advertising pages, the colors will make a nice addition to the mask, but make sure the pages are newsprint, not high-gloss paper.
2. Close the sheets at the fold. Working from the fold down, tear each sheet into strips about 1 inch wide. Set the newspaper strips aside.
3. Begin the paste by mixing the flour and sugar in a big pot or double boiler.
4. Stirring constantly, add the warm water a little at a time. With a wooden spoon, stir vigorously to make a smooth paste with no lumps.
5. Put the pot over medium heat, and stir constantly until the paste is thick and clear and pearly.

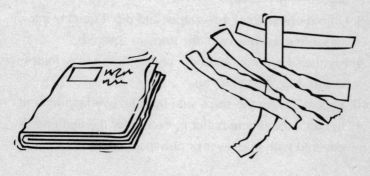

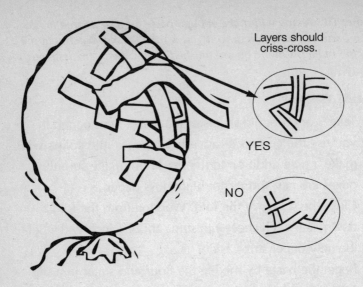

Layers should criss-cross.

YES

NO

6. Remove the paste from the heat, add the cold water, and stir. Let it cool for about five minutes. It should be about the consistency of yogurt.

7. Inflate the balloon and tie the end. You can set the balloon, tied end down, in an empty glass to hold it in place while you work.

8. Unfold one strip of newspaper and dip it quickly into the paste so both sides of the strip are covered.

9. Lay the strip on the balloon, and smooth out wrinkles and folds as best you can.

10. Repeat, laying the strips side by side, overlapping a little, until the whole balloon, except for the tied end, is covered with one layer of newspaper.

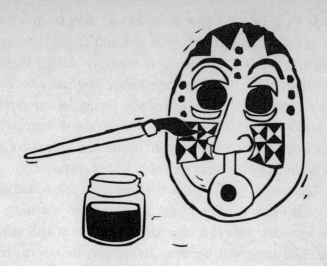

11. Apply a second layer of strips, crisscrossing the first. Continue until you have 5 or 6 layers of crisscrossing strips on the balloon.

12. Let the papier-mâché sit for 2 or 3 days. When it is completely dry, burst the balloon by sticking it with a pin or needle at the tied end.

13. If you want, you can make two masks by using scissors to cut the papier-mâché head in half.

14. To make eyes, nose, and a mouth, you can use scissors and cut the papier-mâché. Or you can make these features out of facial tissues dipped in the wheat paste and bonded to the mask before it dries.

15. If you want to paint the mask, use poster paints.

FAMILY HISTORY BOOK AND TAPE

This is a Kwanzaa project that can and should involve the whole family. All you do is interview family members about their lives and memories. You can concentrate on the oldest members of the family, or interview everybody. You can ask questions about the distant past, or focus on a much more recent event. Anything you do will be worthwhile, and probably full of surprises.

Take notes during the interview or ask someone else to do this while you ask questions. If you have a tape recorder, you can tape the interview at the same time. The tape will become an instant heirloom, because it records how people actually sound, not just what they say.

WHAT YOU NEED:

> notebook
> tape recorder and blank tapes

WHAT YOU DO:

1. Ask people in the family if you may talk with them, and make an appointment for the interview. Arrange to meet with people one or two at a time, for about an hour. Some interviews will take less time, and some will take more.

2. Think about your questions in advance. The first few questions could cover basic facts, such as: When were

you born, and where? What were your parents' names? When were you married? It is good to have this information on record, because these details are easily lost over time. Answering these questions also helps people relax at the beginning of an interview.

In the best interviews, people just talk and tell stories. Once you have asked your basic questions, move on to more open-ended questions to get people started. For example: What is your earliest memory? What were your parents like? What was it like when you were young? How did you meet your husband or wife? You can ask about school, games children played, bedrooms, favorite clothes, holidays, food, sad events and happy ones.

For some people, one question triggers a series of memories, and the stories keep coming. Other people do not remember so easily, or feel a little uncomfortable being interviewed, and your questions will help them. Come prepared with several different kinds of questions, even though you may not need them.

It's better to follow up on the interesting things people say than to cover all your questions.

3. Have everything all set up when you get together for the interview. You might want old family photographs on hand, or other family mementos. If you are taping the interview, put a blank tape in and set the recorder near where you and the person will sit. Test it to make sure

it's picking up the voices.

4. Tape recorders sometimes make people nervous. When you start the interview, turn on the machine, and then ignore it until you need to turn the tape.

5. Rewrite or type your notes and put them together with old family photographs. You can bind them in a beautiful handmade book (see the directions on the following pages), or just put everything in a loose-leaf notebook.

6. If you have made a tape of your interview, label it with the date and the names of the people asking and answering questions. If you want, you can have copies made by a recording service. You might want to put the original into an envelope and keep it with the family-history book. Then, every Kwanzaa, you can bring your family history, read it and listen to it, and make additions.

HANDMADE BOOK

You can use this handmade book for your family history. Or you might make a book of blank pages, cover it with a beautiful fabric in Kwanzaa colors, and ask your guests to write a message in honor of the holiday. However you choose to use the book, it is a very satisfying project to work on as a family, and a wonderful, lasting gift.

WHAT YOU NEED:

> sheets of 8 ½ x 11 blank paper, or a document you want to bind
> 2 sheets of rigid cardboard, 8 ¾ x 11 ½ inches
> large needle
> heavy thread
> medium-weight fabric
> white glue
> cloth or adhesive tape, or translucent plastic tape
> scissors
> ruler

WHAT YOU DO:

1. If you are binding blank pages, go to step 2. If you are binding your family history or another document, the left margin should be wider than usual, or about 1 ½ inches. Add a title page with whatever information you want to record about the book, such as the date or people's names. Put one blank page on top of the title

page, and one blank page at the end of the book.

2. With a large needle and heavy thread, sew the pages together about ¼ inch from the left edge. If you have too many pages to sew, staple the book together.

3. Put one sheet of cardboard on top of the pages and one sheet under them, so the left edges of the pages and the cardboard line up. At the top, bottom, and right edges, the cardboard will extend beyond the pages.

4. Tape the two pieces of cardboard together.

5. Open the book and remove the sewn pages.

6. Lay the two sheets of cardboard on the table so the tape is taut and the cardboard sheets are parallel to each other. This will form a rectangle that is about 18½ x 11½. The exact dimensions will depend on the number of pages in your book.

7. Cut a rectangle of fabric 1 inch wider and longer than

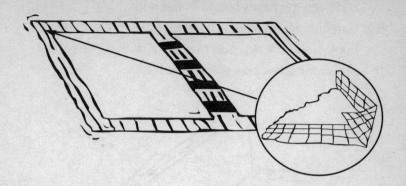

the cardboard rectangle, or about 19½ x 12½.

8. Brush a thin layer of white glue over the surface of the cardboard sheets, and another thin layer on the wrong side of the fabric. Lay the fabric out, glue side up. Carefully center the cardboard sheets, glue side down, on the fabric, and press them into place.

9. Brush a thin layer of white glue on the 1-inch border of fabric beyond the cardboard.

10. Turn one corner of the fabric diagonally over the corner of the cardboard. Repeat for all four corners. Then press the fabric down between the corners. Try to avoid wrinkles.

11. Glue the top blank page to the inside of the front cover. Glue the last blank page to the inside of the back cover. This will hide the glued edge of the fabric,

and keep the pages bound in the book.

12. Carefully remove any spilled glue. Then close the book, and let it dry. You may set it under a heavy flat object for a few hours, so it lies flat.

QUILT

If you have some sewing experience, you can make this long-lasting gift for someone special. These directions will make a quilt that is 45 x 60 inches, a perfect size for a lap quilt or a crib. The pattern, called a charm block, is one of the easiest to make.

New cotton material or scraps from the sewing basket or squares from worn clothing can all be used to make the quilt. You need a total of 108 squares of fabric, each 5½ inches square. You may alternate light and dark colors, or use shades of similar colors, or play with different prints. If you are working on a careful design, plan it out in advance so you cut the right number of squares from each piece of fabric.

WHAT YOU NEED:

brown paper bag
prewashed fabric
iron
#2 pencil or sewing chalk
ruler
pins
45 inch x 60 inch piece of muslin for lining
46 inch x 61 inch nylon batting
(not cotton, which tends to wad up)
needle
yarn
embroidery thread
sewing machine

WHAT YOU DO:

1. Measure and cut an exact 5½ inch square of paper from the brown bag. This is the pattern, or template, for the cloth squares.
2. Press the fabric on the wrong side.
3. Pin the template to the wrong side of the fabric, and trace the square with a #2 pencil or sewing chalk. Repeat, tracing squares until you have the number you need from that piece of fabric. (You can fold the fabric once, so for every square you trace, you cut two layers of fabric. But do not try to cut more than two layers of fabric at a time, as the measurements will not be precise.)
4. Cut the squares out carefully, and stack like-fabric squares together.
5. Working on the floor or a large table, lay the squares out in rows, alternating light and dark cloth. You should have 12 rows of 9 squares each. Study the pattern you see, and make any changes you want.
6. Restack the squares in order, making 9 stacks of 12 squares each. Do this carefully to maintain the pattern you want.
7. Take the top 2 squares from the first stack, and put them right sides together. With the sewing machine, stitch them together along one side with a ¼-inch seam allowance.
8. Continue until you have sewn the stack together into a row of 12 squares.

9. Now sew the second stack together as you did the first. Repeat until you have 9 sewn rows of 12 squares each.

10. Press the rows on the wrong side, with the seams all going in the same direction.

11. Lay the rows out on the floor in order, upside down. You will be able to see the colors, and rearrange the pattern if you want.

12. Pin the rows together, and then stitch them with the sewing machine. Try to line up the corners exactly.

13. Press the sewn squares on the wrong side, with the seams going in the same direction.

14. Press the lining fabric on the wrong side. Pin the lining to the quilt top, and very carefully cut the lining to the same size as the quilt. Put both aside.

15. Working on a clean surface, lay the lining out flat, wrong side up. Then lay on the batting, which will be slightly larger than the lining. Then put on the quilt, right side up. This makes a sandwich with the lining and quilt top on the outside, and the batting in the middle.

16. Using embroidery thread and a large needle, make long basting stitches from the center of the quilt straight across to each of the four edges, forming an X. This will keep the quilt straight and together while you work.

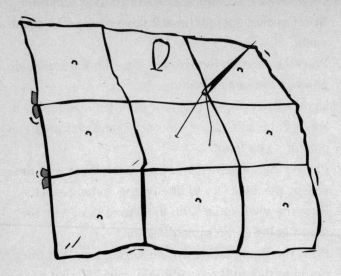

17. Now for the finishing stitch. Thread a large needle with colorful yarn. Push the needle up from the lining side to appear at the center of a square. Then push the needle back through to the lining side, leaving a small loop of yarn visible on the square.

18. On the lining side, tie the yarn in a knot just tight enough not to pucker the fabric. Cut the two ends of yarn so they are no longer than 1 inch.

19. Repeat, until you have a yarn knot in the enter of each square of the quilt.

20. Remove the basting stitches. Carefully trim the batting to about ¼ inch smaller than the quilt top and lining.
21. Turn under the raw edges of the lining and quilt top, pin them together, and hand-stitch the quilt top, lining, and batting together.

FOODS

Prepare these dishes with a parent or with your parent's permission. It is good to start cooking in an uncluttered place, with clean hands and clean utensils. I like to wash a used utensil as soon as I'm done with it, so that at the end of the project I don't have many left to wash. Remember to read all the directions before you start to work. Make sure you have all the ingredients you will need.

PEANUT-AND-RICE PUDDING

Here is a dish from The Gambia, West Africa. Makes 4 servings.

WHAT YOU NEED:

 ½ cup roasted unsalted peanuts
 1 cup uncooked rice
  blender, or 2 pieces of clean cloth
  saucepan or double boiler
 ½ cup peanut butter
 2 cups water
  sugar or honey to taste
  cinnamon or vanilla (optional)

WHAT YOU DO:

1. Blend the rice and peanuts in a blender until they are

mealy. If a blender is not available, place rice and peanuts between 2 pieces of clean cloth and pound until mealy.

2. Mix peanut butter and water thoroughly in a saucepan and bring to a boil.

3. Add rice and peanuts. Cook over low heat or in a double boiler, stirring frequently. Add more water if necessary. Cook until rice is done.

4. Sweeten to taste with sugar or honey. A dash of cinnamon or vanilla may be added.

BENNE WAFERS

Here is another recipe for your file of African dishes.
Makes 50 wafers.

WHAT YOU NEED:

- 1 cup sesame seeds
- skillet
- cookie sheet
- 1 cup light brown sugar, lightly packed
- 4 tablespoons butter, slightly softened
- electric mixer or wooden mixing spoon
- large mixing bowl
- 1 egg, lightly beaten
- ½ cup whole-wheat flour
- ¼ teaspoon salt
- ⅛ teaspoon baking powder
- 1 teaspoon fresh lemon juice
- ½ teaspoon vanilla

WHAT YOU DO:

1. Preheat oven to 325°.
2. Toast the sesame seeds in a large, unoiled skillet over a medium flame for about ten minutes or until they are golden brown. Transfer the seeds onto a cookie sheet and set in a cool place.
3. Using an electric mixer or a wooden spoon, mix the sugar and butter together in a large bowl until they are creamy.

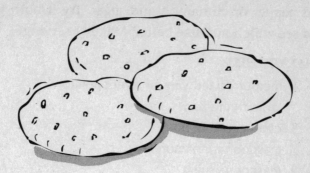

4. Mix flour, salt, and baking powder in another bowl. Add the egg and dry ingredients to creamed sugar and butter, and mix them in thoroughly.

5. Using a wooden spoon, stir in the sesame seeds, lemon juice, and vanilla. Mix well.

6. Drop teaspoons of dough about 1 inch apart onto a well-greased cookie sheet or pan. Bake for 15 minutes or until brown at the edges.

7. Let the wafers cool for 2 minutes, then transfer them to a rack or plate to cool completely.

YAM CHIPS

This African-American dish is delicious with either salt and pepper or cinnamon and sugar. Try it both ways and see which you like better. Makes 1 serving.

WHAT YOU NEED:

- 1 medium-sized yam or sweet potato
  large frying pan
- ¼ cup vegetable oil
- ¼ teaspoon cinnamon
- 2 teaspoons sugar

WHAT YOU DO:

1. Wash and peel the yam or sweet potato; then slice it into thin slices.
2. Heat the oil in a large frying pan over a medium flame for about ten minutes or until a bead of water sizzles when dropped in the oil. (Be careful not to toss too much water into the hot oil.)
3. Fry the potato slices in the hot oil, turning until they cook on both sides to a crisp and golden brown.
4. Drain the chips on paper towels. While they are still hot, sprinkle them with sugar and cinnamon or, if you prefer, with salt and pepper.

AMBROSIA

This recipe is a colorful and delicious addition to a festive occasion. Makes 4 servings.

WHAT YOU NEED:

- 4 large oranges
- 2 cups unsweetened shredded coconut
- ¼ cup sugar
- lettuce leaves (optional)
- whipped cream or non-dairy whipped topping

WHAT YOU DO:

1. Peel the oranges and cut them into ¼ inch slices, removing any seeds.
2. Combine the oranges, coconut, and sugar in a bowl, mixing them gently so as not to break the orange slices.
3. Chill the mixture in the refrigerator for at least ½ hour.
4. You may arrange lettuce leaves on a platter and spoon the mixture onto the leaves if desired.
5. Serve with whipped cream or non-dairy whipped topping.

SWAHILI GLOSSARY AND PRONUNCIATION KEY

A note about pronunciation: Swahili is written in a form of the Arabic alphabet. This pronunciation guide is based upon Roman alphabet transliterations.

Swahili vowels are pronounced as follows:

> a = like the *a* in c*a*r
> e = like the *eh* in h*eh*
> i = like the *ee* in f*ee*
> o = like the *o* in g*o*
> u = like the *oo* in m*oo*

The consonants are pronounced the same as they are in English. The *g* in *gele* is hard, like the *g* in go. The *m* in *mkeka* is pronounced like the *em* in emerald. The *n* in *nguzo* is pronounce like the *en* in end. The accent is almost always on the next-to-last syllable.

AFRICAN GARMENTS

BUI-BUI (BOOEE-booee): Elegant robe or gown for women

BUSUTI (boo-SOO-tee): Robe with a scarf at the waist

DASHIKI (dah-SHEE-kee): A loosely fitting shirt for boys and men; a loosely fitting blouse for girls and women

GELE (GEH-leh): Head wrap (West African, not Swahili)

KANZU (KAHN-zoo): Robe for men (West African, not Swahili)

RITUAL SYMBOLS OF KWANZAA

KIKOMBE CHA UMOJA
(kee-KOHM-bee chah oo-MOH-jah): Unity cup

KINARA (kee-NAH-rah): Candle holder

MAZAO (mah-ZAH-oh): Crops

MKEKA (em-KEH-kah): Woven mat

MISHUMAA SABA (mee-shoo-MAH-ah SAH-bah): Seven candles

VIBUNZI (vee-BOON-zee): Ears of corn

ZAWADI (zah-WAH-dee): Gifts

THE SEVEN PRINCIPLES OF KWANZAA:

IMANI (ee-MAH-nee): Faith

KUJICHAGULIA (koo-jee-chah-GOO-lee-ah): Self-determination

KUUMBA (koo-OOM-bah): Creativity

NIA (NEE-ah): Purpose

UJAMAA (oo-jah-MAH-ah): Cooperative economics

UJIMA (oo-JEE-mah): Collective work and responsibility

UMOJA (oo-MOH-jah): Unity

SWAHILI WORDS AND PHRASES
USED FOR KWANZAA

BENDERA (behn-DEH-rah): Flag

HABARI GANI (hah-BAH-ree GAH-nee):
What's the news?

HARAMBEE (hah-RAHM-beh): A call to unity and
collective struggle—to pull together

KARAMU (kah-RAH-moo): Feast

KIKOMBE (kee-KOHM-beh): Cup

KWANZA (KWAHN-zah): First

KWANZAA (KWAHN-zah): An African-American
holiday that begins on December 26 and ends on
January 1. It is a time when African-Americans
gather together to celebrate themselves and their
history. The extra *a* is added to make the word
seven letters long to symbolize the seven principles and days of Kwanzaa.

KWANZAA YENU IWE HERI
(KWAHN-zah YEH-noo EE-weh HEH-ree): Happy
Kwanzaa!

MATUNDA YA KWANZA
(mah-TOON-dah yah KWAHN-zah): First fruits

MISHUMAA (mee-shoo-MAH-ah): Candles

NGUZO (en-GOO-zoh): Principles

SABA (SAH-bah): Seven

TAMBIKO (tahm-BEE-koh): Pouring drink for
ancestors—a libation

TAMSHI LA TAMBIKO

(TAHM-shee lah tahm-BEE-koh): Statement made when pouring drink for ancestors

TAMSHI LA TUTAONANA

(TAHM-shee lah too-tah-oh-NAH-nah): Statement of farewell

Achebe, Chinua, *Things Fall Apart*. Greenville, CT: Fawcett, 1959.

Anderson, David A., *Kwanzaa: An Everyday Resource and Instructional Guide*. New York: Crumbs and Thomas, 1992.

Brewer, J. Mason, *American Negro Folklore*. Chicago: Quadrangle Books, 1972.

Brewer, J. Mason, *Worse Days and Better Times: Tales of the Wise and Foolish*. Chicago: Quadrangle Books, 1965.

Botkin, B. A., ed., Federal Writing Projects: *Lay My Burden Down: A Folk History of Slavery*. Chicago: University of Chicago Press, 1945.

Bryan, Dianetta, "Her Story Unsilenced: Black Female Activists in the Civil Rights Movement." *Sage* magazine, Vol. 5, #2, Fall 1988.

Copage, Eric, *Kwanzaa: An African American Celebration of Culture and Cooking*. New York: William Morrow, 1991.

Du Bois, W.E. Burghardt, *Black Reconstruction in America*. Cleveland & New York: World Publishing, 1964.

Du Bois, W.E. Burghardt, *Dark Water: Voices from Within the Veil*. New York: Schocken, 1969; new edition, New York: Harcourt Brace, 1975.

Franklin, John Hope, *The Emancipation Proclamation*. New York: Doubleday, 1963.

Hughes, Langston, and Milton Meltzer. *A Pictorial History of the Negro in America*. New York: Crown, 1956-1963.

Hughes, Langston, and Arna Bontemps, eds., *Book of Negro Folklore*. New York: Dodd, Mead, 1958.

Hurston, Zora Neal, *Mules and Men*. Philadelphia: J. B. Lippincott, 1935; new edition, Bloomington, IN: Indiana University Press, 1978.

Karenga, Maulana, *Kwanzaa: Origins, Concepts, Practice*. Los Angeles: Kawaida Publications, 1977.

Karenga, Maulana, *The African American Holiday of Kwanzaa*. Los Angeles: University of Sankore Press, 1988.

Kenyatta, Jomo, *Facing Mt. Kenya*. New York: Vantage Books, 1965.

Madhubuti, Safisha, *The Story of Kwanzaa*. Chicago: Third World Press, 1989.

Mathis, Sharon Bell, *Listen for the Fig Tree*. New York: Viking, 1974.

McClester, Cederic, *Kwanzaa: Everything You Wanted to Know but Didn't Know Where to Ask*. New York: Crumbs & Thomas, 1985-1990.

Musgrove, Margaret, *Ashanti to Zulu*. New York: Dial, 1976.

Porter, A.P, *Kwanzaa*. Minneapolis: Carolrhoda Books, 1991.

Rubel, David, *Fannie Lou Hamer From Sharecropping to Politics*. Englewood, NJ: Silver Burdett, 1990.

Sertima, Ivan Van, ed., *Golden Age of the Moor*. New Brunswick, NJ: Transaction, 1992; second edition, 1993.

Thompson, Helen Davis, *Let's Celebrate Kwanzaa*. New York: Crumbs and Thomas, 1989.

Walter, Mildred Pitts, *Have a Happy*. New York: Lothrop, Lee and Shepard, 1989; paper edition, New York: Avon, 1990.

Walter, Mildred Pitts, *Girl on the Outside*. paper edition, New York: Scholastic, 1993.